ARCTIC BLUES

illustrated by
Peter Lawson

story by
Elizabeth Laird

For John and Joan – P.L.

For William – E.L.

HEINEMANN · LONDON

William Heinemann Ltd., Michelin House, 81 Fulham Road, London SW3 6RB LONDON   MELBOURNE   AUCKLAND
First published 1989   Illustrations copyright © Peter Lawson 1989   Text copyright © Elizabeth Laird 1989   ISBN 434 94743 1
Produced by Mandarin Offset, Printed and bound in Hong Kong   All Rights Reserved

Zippi and Zac were fast asleep.
Samson knocked at the door.
They didn't hear him.
"Good morning," he said.
Zippi and Zac slept on.

"Wakey, wakey!" yelled Samson.
The house shook. The windows rattled.
"What? Who? Don't shoot!" said Zac.
"It's only me," said Samson.
"You're needed at the office."

At the perch, broken ice was everywhere.
"Odd," said Zippi. "It's summertime."
Zac picked up a piece of ice.
A message was scratched on it.
"Come to the North Pole," he read.

"Dropped by a passing puffin, perhaps," said Zippi.
"Mark my words, the Mad Ducks are behind this. Call FIFI. We leave at dawn."
"But dawn was hours ago," said Zac.
"Lunchtime then," said Zippi.
"And don't forget to wear your snowshoes."

Free International Flights Inc arrived at noon.
"Oh no!" said Zac. "I can't."
"You can," said Zippi.
"I shan't," said Zac.
"You must," said Zippi.
"I won't," said Zac.
"You will," said Zippi. "At least it'll be quick."

He strapped Zac to one rocket,
and tied himself to the other.
"Pass me my polar kit," he said to Samson,
"and wish us a soft landing."

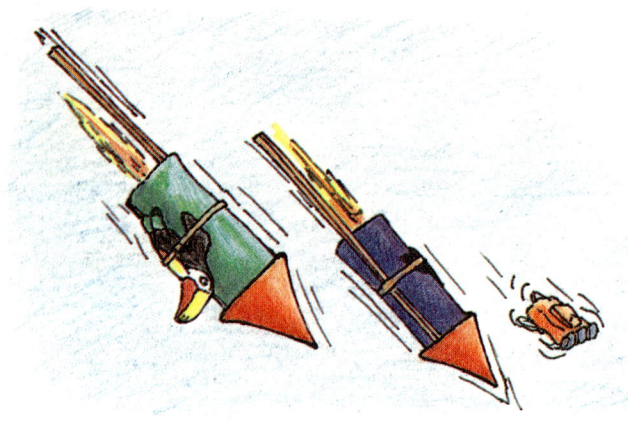

Five minutes later, everything went white.
"I'm dead," wailed Zac. "I know I'm dead!"
"Dead birds don't squawk," said Zippi.
"Come on. Help me find our stuff."

Luckily, the polar kit wasn't far away.
Zippi checked right through it.
"Walrus moustaches, sealing wax, husky throat pills...
Good, it's all in order," he said.

At that moment, a polar bear appeared.

"Wah!" screamed Zac.

"Don't panic," said the bear. "I won't hurt you. Have a nice cold drink."

"How kind," said Zippi. "Two cans, please. One for me and one for my friend."

"Brr," said Zac, when he'd finished his. "That *was* an ice-cold drink."

"Thank goodness you came," said the bear.
"The Mad Ducks flew in a week ago.
They're roaring at the sea lions,
they're getting at the gulls,
and they're eating all the whale's fish."

"What's that awful noise?" said Zac.
"It's the Mad Ducks' pop group," said the bear.
"Quentin and the Quackers."
Zippi put his wings over his ears.

"You're right." he said. "The Mad Ducks must go."
"Hey!" said Zac. "That mountain's moving!"
"It's just a passing iceberg," said the bear.
"It's given me an idea," said Zippi.

He reached into his polar kit.
"Here, Zac," he said.
"Put on this bow tie and play this flute."
"Why me?" said Zac.
"Because you've got class," said Zippi.

Zac played a sonata, a minuet and a trio.
The Mad Ducks booed and hissed.
"'Orrible! Boring! Rubbish!" they screamed.
Even the bear looked disappointed.
"It needs more oomph," he said.

Zippi dug into his kit again.
"Right, Zac," he said.
"Put on this pop star outfit and play this guitar."
"Why can't you do it?" pleaded Zac.
"Because you've got rhythm, baby," said Zippi.

Zac sang a big rock number.
and Zippi used the rockets for drums.
The Mad Ducks went wild.
They screamed, and fainted, and cried.
"More! More!" they chanted.

"OK," said Zippi, "but not here.
Kindly step onto this iceberg, ladies and gentlemen.
It's got a natural stage."

While the Mad Ducks flocked onto the iceberg,
Zippi explained his idea to the polar bear,
who told it to the whale.
"Do you agree?" asked Zippi.
"I don't mind if I do," said the whale.
"It's time I went south,
and anyway, I'll enjoy the music."

Zippi dived into his bag again
and brought out a very long rope.
Zac tried to tie it round the iceberg.
The iceberg was too big.
Zac slipped and bumped his beak.
He said a rude word.

Then he tried to tie it round the whale's tail.
The tail was too slippery.
Zac fell into the icy, arctic sea.
He said another rude word.

"Naughty, naughty," said Zippi. "Stand back, Zac."
He drilled a hole in the iceberg with his beak,
tied the rope through it,
and passed the loop to the whale.

"Pull it with your mouth like a horse," he said.

"What a genius," said the polar bear.

Zippi smiled modestly.

"We aim to please," he said. "OK! Let's go!"

The Mad Ducks were impatient.
"Zippi, Zippi, Zippi! Zac, Zac, Zac!" they roared.
Zac jumped onto the stage and began to sing.
The Mad Ducks screamed with joy.

They didn't see the rope or the whale.
They didn't notice that the iceberg was moving.
They didn't hear the bear shouting,
"Goodbye, and don't come back!"

At the end of an hour, Zippi and Zac were tired.
At the end of two hours, they were hoarse.
At the end of the afternoon, they were exhausted.

When it got dark, they were half-dead.
But the Mad Ducks wouldn't let them stop.
"If this is fame, you can keep it," said Zippi.

When dawn broke, the North Pole was far away.
The Mad Ducks were still hard at it.
"Zippi, Zippi, Zippi! Zac, Zac, Zac!" they yelled.
But Zippi and Zac could only croak.
So the Mad Ducks changed their tune.

"Quentin and the Quackers!" they shouted,
and the gruesome group started up again.
"I can't bear it," whispered Zac.
"You won't have to for long," said Zippi.
"Have you noticed something? The iceberg's melting.
It's half the size it was already."

Suddenly there was a crash.
Everyone fell flat on their faces.
"Shipwreck!" yelled Zac. "SOS! Fire! Police!"
"Relax," said Zippi. "We've landed."
The iceberg had hit an island.
The ducks were delighted.

"Ponds!" they shouted. "Frogs! Duckweed!"
They flew ashore and got busy.
"Can I tow you home?" the whale asked Zippi.
"Sure can, man," said Zippi. "A do-be-do-do."
Zac groaned.
"Cut out the pop star stuff," he said,
"or I'll do my nut."
"Nuts?" said Zippi. "Yes, please."

Back home, Samson was waiting for them.
"Samson!" squawked Zippi. "What's happened to you?"
"I've started a pop group," said Samson.
"Listen to this great little drum routine."
He rapped out a brilliant rhythm on his house.
"Aaagh!" wailed Zippi and Zac together.
"You're jealous," said Samson. "But I sympathize.
Not everyone can be strong and smart and slimy,
like me.